After the Flood Comes th

Naoise Gale

Published by Nine Pens

2021

www.ninepens.co.uk

ISBN: 978-1-8384321-8-8

007

Contents

7 Before You

8 Fruit of her Womb

9 Doctor, Doctor

11 The First Time

14 Dream

15 The Part of Me I Call Nigel

16 Best Friend

18 Breaking the Glass

20 Hospital

22 What I Know About Love

23 Paracetamol

24 Rose

25 In Which Aphrodite is my Agony Aunt

26 Mania

28 Tomorrow

29 Never Detox at Home on a Saturday

31 Memory

33 Autumn

34 A Lesson in Poetry

For my mother,

who always asks the right questions.

Before You

Before I was half-pill and absence,
before I was ice cubes in a tinkling
glass, before I was blue fizz in the
parched afternoon, I was good
girl at the front desk, arm raised
in the air like one thin butter knife.
I was scrawled equations and
poached eggs on toast, oil coating
my gaping mouth; I was dumb
tulips and the hushed gasp
of a teacher: "One-hundred per
cent again". Before shitty
knickers and puked cookies,
I was all there, vibrant, anxiety
girl with her paranoid magic
powers. I was the fizzle of
Diet Coke in my belly and the echo
of skulking words in my mind
and the crunch of an apple
in a perfect, heart-shaped
mouth. Before I was you, I
was me, boring little girl,
arrogant, all pine and Nordic
furniture. Boring little girl,
but myself.

Fruit of her Womb

It is half-baked morning when I shit frogspawn into the
immaculate bowl,
green bile seeping from me like alien matter. My mother is in
the next room
singing to the birds, and my heart is heavy as the weights
I heaved last night while she was pretending to sleep. My
soupy head
aches and there are ketones, pear-drop-sweet, on my tongue.
She says I smell like rotten fruit, like a maggoty thing, like
summer death.
I am sterilised cold, and I moan at her to turn up the heating;
she poaches
the egg yolk sun and serves it up to me at lunchtime,
congealed.
It's funny the way it drips down the wall, but neither of us
laugh.
"Naoise," she says, "You have to eat." Her tone is brittle as
Glacier mints and her voice sucks the air from the room.
Later, I stew in bed as she scrubs slime from the walls, sore
knuckles
bleeding like Wagyu. We do not talk of the incident, but clasp
each other close as two clams within a shell, and the chocolate
night
melts onto us and she is mallow-soft in my arms.

Doctor, Doctor

In late autumn, when the leaves
skittered like ghoulish crisp packets
on the glassy ground, my mother
frogmarched me to the doctor,
muttering lines about
blown blood sugar and gut stained
toilet bowls and breath that smelled
of decay. My cannibal-body wilted
in the small plastic chair, and I
rested my chin on my palm,
like a crumpled sheet of paper. The
doctor was tinkling skirts and woodsmoke,
hippy-dippy middle-class thing; she read
my weight backwards and chimed, "She's as thin
as an ice-pick. Her eyes are haunted." I smirked
and blew pink bubbles into the paused air,
skinny bitch, all woozy pride. Anorexia
was a crass hand on my shoulder, something
to clutch in the night when leg muscles
knotted and stomach complained. We were
a pencil sketch of twisted shadow-hands, two
hands under the desk in the crude classroom,
two sides of the same dark pill. Doctor said,
"Maybe she needs a car," as though the
problem was my location, or my transport,
as though I could drive into the forget-me-not

dusk and eat coffee cake on a bench coated
in tumbleweed, I just needed some wheels,
Goddamnit, some black rubber tyres to coast
me away from this wretched place. After anointed
appointment I cried in the corridor, all white milk
and roses, all freeze-fog, all bruised anger. Then
my mother clutched my bird-palm in hers and we
were two cream hands in the half-light, one dark
hand on the heart.

The First Time

It was early morning, birdsong and breeze, sky the colour of
apricots, when
you took the pill, crunched it under your tongue like a tic tac,
imagining
a minty serenity and strong flavours of euphoria. For weeks
before the
first taste, you had thought of nothing else, only girls with
breath like
air-conditioning units and barbed wire eyes. A clean high,
fresh
as summer grass and eucalyptus. The pill crumbled under
your
bulbous tongue, like a soggy piece of paper in the spring rain,
or
an old bus ticket in a purse. It took two hours to hit: two
hours of
bored television and half-hearted wanking, two hours of
searing
consciousness and numb depression. Two hours of the tip of
a nail scratching your perfect white teeth. But when it arrived,
it was all glory. The sun spun and spat fat orange sparks onto
the lawn. The scrawny cat arched its back and meowed,
pained.
The neighbourhood Alsatian barked a haunted cello suite.
Your legs,

spindly things, became malleable as jelly noodles. They wobbled,

rotten twigs and the scent of decaying wood. Church bells boomed

in the background. Sunset was a spilled glaze, dripping

like melted candy onto the shimmering horizon. You thought of your

mother, and the unanswered texts on your phone, and the assignment

you still had to do and all the chores and all the doubts and your mother,

your mother, your mother and you took more pills. Four, to be precise.

It was strange the way the world unzipped, as though enclosed in God's

handbag. You had never seen the trees bend before, supple as arched

bows, or the clouds fall to the ground like fainting sheep. You had never

known the colour of the wind – the blue of poster paints, a whisker

lighter than indigo – or the sound of dusk falling – Indian pipes, reedy,

with the faint clang of melancholic tambourines. You had not known

that a pill could be a whisper, or a shout, or a guttural scream of

"Fuck you!" to the world, "Fuck all of you and fuck me too!". You had

not known the particular pain of landing, eyes swollen and
sore,
teeth the yellow of literary tomes, and finding your chemical
wings
shattered on the callous ground, flat as pages. You had much
to learn.

Dream

There was a breath of white fog
that smothered the vast mouth
of water like a wet hand; there
was a boy on a canoe pedalling
furiously into the half-smoke;
there was a vase of lilies in the
hallway, drooping into oblivion.
I sat whale-quiet in the doorway,
mind fixed on a peculiar dream:
a sliver of foil silver as mercury,
a straw long and thin, blue smoke
thick as New Delhi smog. Two
teenaged cherubs danced in
my vision, laughing as I inhaled.
The smoke plumed from my
nose like cold breath, and my
cold breath plumed from my
mouth, like smoke. The fog
kept on sighing, and a thousand
other girls like me breathed air
clouded as fresh Italian lemonade.

The Part of Me I Call Nigel

There is something wrong with me. The shrinks
call it bipolar disorder, autism, social anxiety
but that doesn't explain the part of me that
wants to break everything, the part
that glimmers after the apocalypse of a row
with my poor, haunted mother. It does not
explain why I craved withdrawal as much as
the blue smog of opiate surrender, why I
decided to become an alcoholic amidst the
dreamy watercolour of Giudecca, why I
wanted to be abhorrent. Truth is, in the
beginning I wanted attention, but now I'm
ensnared and I want everyone to fuck
right off. This part of me is yellow and fatty
as a diseased liver; it is the damp underside
of a whale's white belly; it is the cannibal
glow of streetlamps at pale summer dusk.
It won't let me be happy. It sends me
scrambling for a fix. Sure, I'm blaming
everything on an invisible particle, but it
is there, I tell you. It told my mother I
wanted to kill myself. Her face was
Papier-Mache in a parade of hankies
and snowballed tissues. And she took
the knife from my hands. And she
threw it down the drain. And the sun
set behind us. And the sun set behind us.

Best Friend

I don't want to write anymore about
my mother's angelic proportions, I
want to write about you, basking
with me in the darkness, in the
dungeon-light of half-baked regret
and half-eaten sorrow. The perfect,
blood-apple heart of the matter is
that you were flawed enough and
frail enough to tell, tallies up your
arms like you were counting lies,
unlike mine, too numerous to
carve into the supple chalkboard
of skin. The sweetest part was that
you asked me if they were prescribed,
such was your trust in me, your Dionysus –
my roundabouts of mood made
you look steady, bumble-bee queen,
next to me you were honey and warm
milk, even when you cut off all your
russet hair and died it chemical toilet
blue. Next to you I was green glass on
a salt-lick shore. Next to you I was needles
and cheap wine. You would never let
me call you up, only messages - was it
to hide the iron drip crimson soak
tap from me, was it to hide the leaky

faucets of your broken wrists? When
you left I was like a raincloud, roaming
and roaming. Everything was white
like the sky and the sea and the snow
and the sun and the pills and your
pale, pale halo. Why did you leave
me, my friend? Why did you leave?

Breaking the Glass

Everything started well, that's what breaks
my pig heart. I didn't mean to break things
but I love the sound of smashing, I love when
shards shower us like clear, sparkling rain,
I love when they shine around us like
cracked ice. Still, I didn't mean to break
the mirror, or the keyboard you lugged into
the corner of the room, or the toilet I clogged
with thick, undigested puke. I didn't mean to
turn the place into a drug den – crushed up,
water-soaked co-codamol in my freezer, busy
separating into a layer of white paracetamol
powder and bitter, opiate-spiked liquid, packets
of pills everywhere, like silver playing cards – I
didn't mean to lay on the floor delirious and
dreaming of poppy-black skies, moons that
spun and purged a spattering of pill-white stars.
I didn't mean to spit blood into the bowl, I didn't
mean to break your heart and mine, glassy-eyed
drive to the hospital, revived with naloxone. I
didn't mean it even though I lit the fire, held
the lighter to the shaky foil, was the foul liar
who broke the stairs and the cupboard and
the house, punched my head with my fist
until I was concussed and the messy room
was a crayon smudge. Even though I sat

amongst the flickering flames, skin
blackened, lips heroin-brown, eyes
golden, and told my mother I was fine.

Hospital

You asked to see my scars
so I unpeeled the sweater
from my arms and displayed
the most immediate ones,
the ones that smiled like
ugly, lipsticked mouths, the
ones that were so bright and
new they looked painted.
A little further down, I fingered
the older scars – brown at first,
like lines of squashed insects,
then razor-white. You asked
why I was here and I stumbled
over my words, muttered
something vague about bulimia
and a four-month-away
psychiatrist appointment. I tricked
you, you see. I pretended that
I was suicidal dandelion – a
flash of eroded teeth and
hacked up limbs, and I was
back out on the streets, under
the useless crisis team. You
forgot about the codeine in
my blood and the blood in
my vomit and the vomit on

my bathroom floor. You forgot
an overdose could be accidental.
I went home and got high, laid
under cotton sheets and
watched *Rolling Stones* concerts
until the sky outside was
black as my torn insides
and the world was muted
enough that all of me breathed –
my scars and my teeth and my
tongue and my poor, bleeding
stomach. The breath slithered
from me like slow, seeping blood.
And I closed my eyes.

What I Know About Love

Do not love me. I am a liar and a fraud, I
will take the glass heart of your love and
smash it against a concrete slat,
let the shards pour down the street
like glistening oil; I will consume you,
stick my dirty fingers down my throat,
puke up your caloric, junk-affection. I
will take your tears – wet pipe – snort
them and smile. You will find me in
your house: in your fractured plates,
your cold coffee, the bathroom
cupboard with the empty tramadol
bottle. Do not love me because
my love hurts for years and years,
it blisters and scalds, it cries on the
powdery sill of a snowstorm overdose.
It screams through sweating withdrawal,
it scratches, it claws. And it laughs. Oh
Jesus, it laughs about drugs. What an
empty, harsh bark. What cruel praise.
My love spoons you in the night, hot
as liquid dope, then turns to the
cold side of the bed, where your
desperate arms cannot reach.

Paracetamol

One day, when the sky was thunderous and threatening, my mother
offered me paracetamol for my headache, passed me a silver packet
flimsier than fairies and said, "I think that's paracetamol. Check it's
not anything dodgy." My bright eyes bugged, you know the way
I mean, like those cartoon eyes, obscenely large, like great shining
eggs in a fresh Caesar salad. My mother, shrill, laughed as high
as violins, "Not that we have any dodgy pills in our house." I
remember, the morning sky was pale as soured cream, and the
bare winter branches stretched like thin, binging fingers. I thought
of jaundiced pills in my pencil case, the homemade one with the
sunset print, and in the Blue Tack, and in my favourite jigsaw puzzle.
I thought of summer glow, orange as resin, and I took the paracetamol
and I took the yellow pills and I was crooner in a snowstorm, crow in
the bruise-black of night.

Rose

She crushes rose petals with a paperweight. Bleeding
perfumed sap – white powder, molten glacier – she
snorts tiny pink fragments small as plastic beads. Girl
becomes rosewater legend, skin pinker than flamingos
or her two-year-old daughter's bedroom walls. Nose
is chapped and leaking raspberry lemonade, sickly
Calpol and dip-dyed lava. Eyes bulge like pastel candy
shrooms and head droops like wilted bud, all sputtered
potential. Girl thinks, 'This is medical. This is sacred,'
before her sugar-veins clog and rupture, like those
roses in a vice, pressed into artistic submission. If
girl is flower power under floral spell, she is
weak as daisy chains when she wakes, in a white
room, no bouquets in sight.

In Which Aphrodite is my Agony Aunt

Dear Aphrodite,
I think I am cursed to lovelessness. Many wars
have been fought over this skin and now the
white wing of a man's hurried fingers feels
like a club to the chest, like a sparrow's beak
poking the soft meat of my thighs. If love is
a delicate thing, I am prone only to shell-
hardness: I am a black swan amongst love's
fresh marine colonies. It's true, sometimes I
imagine myself prone on a sunshine beach,
arm around shoulders, mouth on mouth, blue
shrapnel of sea glimmering beside his neck,
wind on my cheeks, taste of salt and spit. But
I cannot stand their hands, cannot stand their
corkscrew tongues, cannot stand their moist
breath on my ear, cannot stand the searching
pressure of them. I pronounce strange words
on my clean tongue – asexual, aromantic –
and bleed from my unbroken cervix and tell
you, Aphrodite, that I am a frigid, unsociable
cunt of a woman, love me regardless.

Mania

1.   Inflated self-esteem or grandiosity
                    I throw my head back and open
                    my cavernous mouth – a dozen
                    sunset-hued birds fly out, wings
                    filigreed with copper wire, bodies
                    delicate as glass. They shine and sing,

2.   Decreased need for sleep
                    flee into the two-am blackness,
                    into the Halloween-glare of an
                    over-zealous moon. My toes
                    feel like worms in the dirt. The
                    soil is dark as night. I hum to the

3.   Increased talkativeness
                    melody of a wounded wolf, rush
                    back inside to inform my dozing
                    flatmates of the beauty of hushed
                    pre-dawn. At pre-drinks they told
                    me to shut up and down liquor

4.   Racing thoughts
                    but my mouth was a mandibular
                    spewing venom. I told them the
                    stars were like headlights and
                    that technology was a message
                    from God: they called me crazy

5.	Distracted easily

>	and locked me in the kitchen
>	as I stacked their dirty dishes
>	beside the crusted sink. Later,
>	once the screaming was done
>	and the crying was done and

6.	Increase in goal-directed activity or psychomotor
agitation

>	the laughing – God the awful,
>	uncontrollable laughing – was
>	done, they let me out and, like
>	a dog, I bounded into my room
>	and painted thirty ceramic tiles

7.	Engaging in activities that hold the potential for
painful consequences, e.g., unrestrained buying sprees

>	in shrill lemon-print. After cantaloupe
>	dawn, I had sex with the tallest
>	who thumbed my dimples and
>	called me a crazy bitch. It was a
>	strange Wednesday night. Alien-
>	like. One-two-three-four-ten hours
>	endless. Bright.

Tomorrow

Tomorrow you will get clean.
The only sound will be the
church bells of your stunted
apologies and the hiss of your
half-breath and the low knock
of your rattling bones. Tomorrow
you will shit turpentine and
taint the room with the smell
of your drugged sweat; tomorrow
you will be crazed shivers and
rosehip; tomorrow you will
be the watermelon-cool
of a wet cloth on your forehead
and the dust-heat of your sweating,
undulating sheets. Tomorrow you will
curl next to your mother like a
perfect, grinning spoon; tomorrow
you will write poetry about drugs,
lonely girl; tomorrow you will weep
in the tar-black night. You crush
tomorrow under a paperweight,
chop it into thin, perfect lines.
In two tomorrows you will get
clean. Maybe. Perhaps. Never mind.

Never Detox at Home on a Saturday

When I awoke, it was moonless, thank God, because
we've all heard enough about giant aesthetic moons
in wolf-black skies. Crescent moons like
knives and round orbs white as snowy owls,
blah blah blah. I had a headache, not a headache
like toddlers in a library or aimless night traffic, you
understand, a headache like a saw in the skull, or
glass files on a supple beach. It was early hours
of Saturday morning and all the drug counsellors
were in bed with their husbands and their kids and
their hairy, panting dogs. Never detox at home on
a Saturday: there's no suboxone in sight. I was all
loneliness and restless shiver – there's nothing else
to be on a Saturday when the medicine is gone and
the drug counsellors are in their beds. I tried the
answerphone a few times but it was stagnant
as those ponds mosquitoes sup from in summer,
the ones with the frogspawn and the intestinal
parasites. I dreamt of telling my mother about
silver packets and highs like eerie Egyptian sunsets
but I forgot my words as soon as I saw her. My
opiate cleanse was flu-like and clammy; my
mother pressed cool cloths on my forehead
and made me drink water with lemon and honey.
It's funny how it didn't stop the tremors. Maybe
I needed a half-death to wake me from my addiction,

or maybe God was just out that day, busy playing racket-ball with toothless angels and old, withered grannies. Santa Claus was chasing after bad kids, and no one was left for the junkies or the misfits.

Memory

I remember you as lemon-thyme
and scorched grass, endless knives
of wet grass through my wriggling
toes, stinking summer grass dotted
with frail daisies, sunlight that
streamed onto me like melted butter.
I remember the feeling of angel
hair through my clasping fingers,
the webs of early autumn made
iridescent with silvery sunshine;
I remember the sound of police cars
that slapped down oil-wet roads
and unleashed steaming sirens.
I remember the occasional clench
of my fists around private stashes
in the semi-darkness of illegal nights,
I remember highs like sanguine
Sudanese sunrises, I remember
every drip of you on the molten
carpet, I remember the bitter
taste of you on my tongue, I
remember I remember I remember.
I cannot forget. Dreams like pink
bridal shrouds haunt me – these nights
I am always laid flat with a palmful
of pills, butter-soft on the carpet,

never hacking blood into
the toilet, or passing out as my
desperate mother slaps my blue-
tinged cheek in a taxi to the hospital.
I am never explaining myself to
judgemental staff, or sitting stiff in
a room marked 'OD', naloxone
still noisy and abhorrent in my
veins. No, in my memory it is
always summer, and we twist
together like a daisy chain, weak
as anything, but oh so beautiful.

Autumn

Days like this when lightning
smacks the grey cheek of sky,
I want to use so much my
teeth hurt. I see an alternative
autumn in my third constricted
eye – maple leaves and bald
birches, robins that bob childlike
in the serene breeze, occasional
whiteness that fills the earth
with pill cleanliness. I want to
sink and never emerge; I want
to close my lids and let
consciousness fester in some
other poor soul. There is an
insect on my desk which
irks me but I cannot kill. I
am a feast of greyness in
the drizzly afternoon. Do
not talk to me in absolutes.
I can only see haze clearly.
I can only see a girl with
a needle and thread.
I can only see the needle,
star-bright. I cannot
see the stars. Open my eyes.

A Lesson in Poetry

All my poems start something like this:
praise be to pills and soft opium tentacles!
Holy ghost of childhood promise be damned,
sing me eery autumn lullabies about women
with skyscraper irises, pocketfuls of pink sand.
Turn down the volume and let peace play
like radio interference. Usually, at this point,
I talk about my mother, two-bit part, more
resilient than iron boots, and I paint you
a delirious fuchsia sunrise, fuzzy as floss.
Something about spoons, metal music.
The feeling of nausea before it bursts.
Venetian high tide, laughing men in deep
rubber wellies. Bliss that unpeels like
an onion. And some more. A little more.
I would really like to write about something else.

Acknowledgements:

Before You – Anti Heroin Chic
Fruit of her Womb – Shortlisted in the Poetry Space
Competition 2020
Doctor, Doctor – Rabid Oak
The First Time – Ink Sac
Rose – Anti Heroin Chic
Tomorrow – Runner up in Parkinson's Art Poetry
Competition 2020
Memory – Opia Lit
Autumn – Anti Heroin Chic